In the Shadow of God

Joann B. Farlow

Kingdom Builders Publications LLC

© 2020 Joann Farlow
In the Shadow of God
Kingdom Builders Publications, LLC

All rights reserved. No part of this book may be reproduced or transmitted in any form or by any means without written permission from the author.

Printed in the USA

ISBN 978-0-578-65286-3 Soft Cover

Authored by
Joann B. Farlow

Editor
Wanda Brown
Kingdom Builders Publications

Cover Design
LoMar Designs

This Book Belongs to

ACKNOWLEDGMENTS

I thank God for inspiring me to write this book. Apart from the guidance of the Holy Spirit, I can do nothing. To God be all the glory and honor for what He has done and continues to do in my life. I now understand clearly how the books of the Bible were written by God's inspiration. It is awesome to be in a personal relationship with God and hear Him speak.

I thank and praise God for my loving and supporting husband, Samuel, and our six daughters, Latashua, Samantha, JoSondra, Angeline, Ashley, and Keyonia, who are my greatest fans in all my many endeavors. I feel that God gives us children in order to keep us humble, and prayerful at all time. Also, I appreciate my three sons-in-law for their love and support.

Most importantly, I thank God for my precious eight grandchildren. I want my grandchildren to remember me as the Bible describes Timothy's grandmother, Lois. *"I am reminded of your sincere faith, which first lived in your grandmother Lois and in your mother Eunice and, I am persuaded, now lives in you also."* (2 Timothy 1:5).

I thank God for my parents (deceased) who nurtured and prayed for me when I did not know the power of prayer. My seven brothers (one deceased, Bernard), and four sisters (one deceased, Catherine), whom I adore and love very much. Each one of them has blessed me in their own way. Finally, my many nieces, nephews, sisters-in-law, brothers-in-law, cousins, and dear friends, I love you all.

I'm grateful for my former church family at St. Peter A.M.E. Church, Cameron, South Carolina, who helped build my spiritual foundation to help me be the woman I am today.

I'm thankful for my current pastor, Reverend Jerome Anderson, who licensed and ordained me under his leadership. I'm also thankful for Pastor Jerome & Rev. Tina Anderson, of Unity Fellowship Community Church, Orangeburg, SC, who pour so much of their heart, time, love, and, leadership into the members of this great church, praying and interceding for each of us daily. They are teaching and walking as true examples for us to follow. I truly thank God for how I have been blessed under their guidance and leadership.

Finally, I thank two women of God, Carolyn Patricia Thomas (deceased), and Dorothy K. Richardson who have assisted me in my spiritual walk. When I was a babe in Christ, I witnessed their lives reflect their biblical belief and practice as they walked in God's shadow, being an example for me of a walking Bible. They both mentored me and emulated Jesus through their lifestyle. I knew I could live the Christ-like life because they were living it. These are two of the humblest people I have ever met. They both epitomized what a disciple should be. I am blessed to have had them as my friends, family and spiritual sisters of encouragement in the gospel.

FOREWORD

I pray that this book will be a blessing to each of you as you read and experience God's great power and love for you. I pray that the Holy Spirit will speak through you as He has never done. I pray our Heavenly Father stirs up your spiritual gifts and gives you a burning desire to form an intimate relationship with Him. If you have already established your relationship with Him, then I pray that you will experience a deeper one at a higher level.

God had His reasons for inspiring me to write this book. It was already predestined to be a blessing to you if you are reading this text. This is God's book, not mine, He told me what to put on these pages. My way of glorifying Him is merely by walking in obedience. He is the author and finisher of my faith.

CONTENTS

	Acknowledgments	iv
	Foreword	vi
	Introduction	viii
1	CHARACTER IS DEVELOPED IN A STORM	11
2	TAKE COVER – WE ARE UNDER ATTACK	19
3	DON'T BE CONSUMED BY THE STORM	23
4	PERSONAL TESTIMONY ON WAITING ON THE LORD	28
5	WALKING TO THE BEAT OF A DIFFERENT DRUMMER	30
6	PEACE IN THE STORM	33
7	WORSHIP GOD WHILE GOING THROUGH THE STORM	37
8	WAITING ON THE LORD IN THE MIDST OF THE STORM	41
9	REJOICE IN THE LORD	46
10	DESTINED TO WALK IN THE SPIRIT	51
11	I HAD TO EXERCISE THE FOLLOWING VIRTUES	57
	ABOUT THE AUTHOR	59

INTRODUCTION

In the Shadow of God is a work inspired by God. Seven months earlier while praying, God instructed me to write this manuscript. Of course, for whatever reason, I didn't act immediately, so God spoke to me a second time. I began penning my thoughts. I was careful to ask the Lord what was His desired topic and title of the book. Several days later, early November 2002, He answered promptly one sabbath morning while in intercessory prayer at church. God gave me this title. He said, "Remember My shadow in the parking lot? That is to be the book's title." I was blown away. God took away all excuses I could use *not* to write this book. So I went with it and followed His lead.

I reflected back to a Saturday morning in April 2002 in the parking lot of my church where seven members of our evangelism team assembled together, holding hands before disbursing for street ministry. While standing there, I felt a shadow come over me. The tone of that sensation felt overwhelming so much so that for a moment I was somewhat afraid to open my eyes. The power of the Holy Spirit hovered over me. Can you imagine feeling a shadow covering you when your eyes are closed? I didn't know what was happening at the moment, but I knew God was at work in my life. I realized later the revelation that His shadow was a covering over me. He assured me that as long as I stayed under His shadow, He would always be my refuge. God was equipping me to participate with Him for His will in my life. The journey would be extraordinary.

As a little girl growing up on my parents' farm in the rural town of Cameron, South Carolina, I often played outside with my sisters, brothers, and cousins. On sunny days when I saw my shadow I would try to outrun it, but no matter how fast I ran, I could not get away from it. What a blessed assurance to know God is always there. *He will never leave us nor forsake us* (**Joshua 1:5**). We can't outrun Him or His goodness. He keeps us protected from the adversary. *He that dwelleth in the secret place of the highest shall abide under the shadow of the Almighty* (**Psalm 91:1**).

On our Christian walk, we should remember God is always with us. However, there will be times when we will experience great trial and tribulation and not sense God's presence. The spirit of loneliness and abandonment could at those times, attack, but God says, nothing can separate us from His love. That still holds true!

Jesus may have experienced a similar feeling in the Garden of Gethsemane when He undertook the sins of the world on His shoulders. He said to God three times, let this cup pass from me. *And at the ninth hour Jesus cried with a loud voice, saying, Eloi, Eloi, lama sabachthani? which is, being interpreted, My God, my God, why hast thou forsaken me?* (**Mark 15:34**).

Perhaps Jesus was not literal when He thought His Father was forsaking Him, but dreaded the separation. Sin is evil and represents darkness. Sin cannot be in the presence of God. Jesus knew once He took on the sins of the world, there would be a separation from the Father, and that's why the plea was made. (**Matthew 27:46**) *And about the ninth hour Jesus cried with a loud voice, saying, Eli, Eli, lama sabachthani? that is to say, My God, my God, why hast thou forsaken me?*

Initially, I faced difficult situations at the time I started writing this book. I used Jesus' words, *"Let this cup pass from me."* While that sounded deep and spiritual, I realized a time later, I was literally asking God to stop His plan and purpose for my life. When we go through turbulence, we shouldn't ask God to get us out of the storm, rather to give us strength to endure until we are out on the other side a victor. Thank God for the faith, strength, and determination to endure, but not without cost. During those times, I had to seek His face in prayer, day and night. If we abide in God, His wings of protection overshadows us. Everything we go through or will go through, Jesus has already done it, and won us the victory. He gave us the confidence that He overcame the world. He did it well over 2,000 years ago for you and me!

Since that day in the church's parking lot I have never been the same. God took me through a journey of spiritual maturity which led me to a deeper faith walk. He's teaching me how to become obedient, increased my faith in Him, and showed me how much He loves me. Be encouraged in knowing that God is the only one who will always love us, unconditionally and without measure. *"Being confident of this very thing, that he which had begun a good work in you will perform it until the day of Jesus Christ,"* **(Philippians 1:6).**

CHARACTER IS DEVELOPED IN A STORM
Character: Galatians 5:22-23
Chapter 1

Believers must realize that once we are saved God initiates the calling He has on our lives, but our character must be developed to match the assignment. It then becomes our responsibility to exemplify the characteristics of God. The journey begins for us to participate in fulfilling the assignment God has predestined. It is then through trials and life experiences that God begins to prepare us for our assignment. God told Jeremiah, *"Before you were born, even before the foundation of the world I set you apart; I sanctified, and appointed, you as a prophet to the nations"* **(Jer. 1:5).** Ultimately, one day Jeremiah became aware of His divine appointment. God does the same for every believer to get us on task for our life purpose.

The book of **James 1: 1-4** states, "Consider it nothing but joy, my brothers and sisters, whenever you fall into various trials. Be assured that the testing of your faith through experience produces endurance leading to spiritual maturity, and inner peace. Don't be surprised when you go through some trials which will test your faith which produces spiritual maturity. And let endurance have its perfect result and do a thorough work, so that you may be perfect and completely developed in your faith, lacking in nothing." We go through different types of storms in order for God to develop our character. Some storms may be the attack of the enemy and some are self-inflicted. The purpose of the storms are not to hurt us, but in the experiences, God can build our character once we surrender our will to His. God created us to have fellowship with Him through a personal relationship because He loves us so much. Through our relationship with God we understand **1 Corinthians 1:9** that says, "For God is faithful through whom you were called into Fellowship with His Son Christ Jesus." This fellowship with God the Father, must come through His Son, Jesus. There is no other way. God wants fellowship with us, not because of who we are, but because of who He is.

It is only through relationship with Him that will allow us to look more like God. Our hearts, mind, and our lifestyle must be transformed into the image of Jesus. In **Romans 12:2,** The Apostle Paul explained to the Romans what it meant to live the Christian life, *"And be not conformed to this world: but be ye transformed by the renewing of your mind, that ye may prove what is that good, and acceptable, and perfect, will of God."* Paul wanted to make it clear that they cannot live the Christian life without their character being transformed.

When our spiritual understanding is enlightened through the revelation of who God is through His word, then our spiritual eyes become opened. For example, when we experience God's unconditional love while we're going through a situation, we begin to see God's character of love. When we experience God as loving, it teaches us that we should show the same character of love toward others. Through loving others our character of love is developed. As we learn and experience the many characteristics of God, it makes conformity to His character easier.

As Christians, sometimes we think we are one place in our walk with God, but we are not; that is what God had to show me. I knew I had faith going into my spiritual battle because I had the measure of faith that I obtained through salvation, according to **Romans 12:3,** *"For I say, through the grace given unto me, to every man that is among you, not to think of himself more highly than he ought to think; but to think soberly, according as God hath dealt to every man the measure of faith."* One of God's characteristics is that He is omniscience, meaning He is all-knowing. He knows everything and oftentimes He allows us to go through experiences so we can discover spiritual reality. This storm revealed my faith was superficial. God knows that undeveloped faith will not lead us to victory in the battles of life.

Faith is another one of God's characteristics that had to be developed in me. God allowed me to go through trials to develop my faith. Our faith is really tested when we go through a storm and think we are about to lose everything. Until we are in a place where we can't trust anything but God and His word, our character of faith cannot be developed! This is when we surrender ourselves and our will, and we enter into a state of brokenness. We recognize that only God can bring us through the storms. Character is developed in tough times.

We recognize in our brokenness, that we must enter into The Potter's House that Jeremiah spoke of in **Jeremiah 18:1-6**, "This is the word that came to Jeremiah from the LORD: Go down to the potter's house, and there I will give you my message. So I went down to the potter's house, and I saw him working at the wheel. But the pot he was shaping from the clay was marred (flawed, blemish) in his hands; so the potter formed it into another pot, shaping it as seemed best to him. Then the word of the LORD came to me: O house of Israel, can I not do with you as this potter does?" declares the LORD. "Like clay in the hand of the potter, so are you in my hand, O house of Israel."

In my trial I was broken. I was as clay and God took me to the Potter's House to mold and make me more in His image. God, through His Almighty hands, put me back together again. I could not be molded until I got to the point where I cried out, "Not my will Lord, but your will be done." What I did not know at that time was character building was developing me for my assignment.

The reason why some of you are not experiencing victory in your storm is that you are still trying to handle the problem your way. Pray to God, trust Him as the omniscient God He is, all-knowing, faithful and loving and allow Him to shape your character into His image. **Ephesians 2:9-10** tells us, *"Not of works, lest any man should boast. For we are his workmanship, created in Christ Jesus unto good works, which God hath before ordained that we should walk in them."* Man cannot boast in his own abilities, because we are created by God and God alone. In this new creation, God designed us for good works that we should glorify Him by our conversation and our determination to live holy. The Apostle Paul wrote in **Romans 12:2**, *"I beseech you therefore, brethren, by the mercies of God, that ye present your bodies a living sacrifice, holy, acceptable unto God, which is your reasonable service."*

In **2 Peter 1:5-7**, Peter laid out seven Christian characteristics that we ought to pursue: *faith, knowledge, self-control, perseverance, godliness, kindness, and love.* More importantly, these are seven of the character traits of God. If we are to be Christ-like, then we must take on the character of Christ. Peter wrote about the kind of person the Christian should strive to become. If we are honest with ourselves, we will agree there are flaws in our character which need fixing. There are too many people saying God use me, increase my territory. However, when God begins the process of building their character they give up because they don't want to endure the trial.

Though your appointment and my appointment will be different from Jeremiah's appointment, all will be just as important in the bigger scheme of things. Are you aware of your divine assignment? We need to discover our purpose. Ask yourself, why did God Almighty create me ? How can I help to advance God's eternal kingdom?

I realized that instead of asking God what our purpose is, we should be asking God to build our character so we can walk in our purpose.

Once our character is built, we will begin to walk in divine purpose. Our gifts can only carry us to places, but character will keep us there. In Genesis 41 we see Joseph used his gift of interpreting dreams, but God had to develop his character before his ultimate assignment.

God wants us to know Him, trust Him, and to come to a closer understanding of His ways. Our creator wants us to know His character, so He might form our character into His likeness. Christians are not to be imitators or look like the world, but we should look like our Father, our creator. God can only use those who are willing to allow Him to do a character transformation.

Therefore, we must be in right relationship with Him. You also must be willing to go through life's storms to get to your transformation. Genesis 1:26 says, *"Let us make mankind in our image."* God wants to shape our character so we will look more like Him. *God wants us to mature in the fruit of the spirit which contains love, joy, peace, longsuffering, gentleness, goodness, faith, meekness, and temperance* (Galatians 5:22). We can attain the attributes of this fruit by spending time with God, studying, applying His word, and staying connected to our source. In **John 15:1-2,** Jesus said, *"I am the true vine, and my Father is the husbandman. Therefore, if we are the branches connected to the vine we should be bearing fruit."* When we confess to be a Christian we should see Christ like behavior being displayed in our life. According to John 15:5, *"If a man remains in me and I in him, he will bear much fruit; apart from me you can do nothing."*

God is omnipotent, which is another one of His characteristics, meaning all-powerful. We must rely on the power of God as we go through our daily lives. Some Christians go through the same problems or situations over and over because they do things out of their own strength, instead of relying on the power of God. So many are depressed, frustrated, sad, angry, complaining, or blaming others for their problems, because they are not willing to trust the power of

God. We must go through the character-building process. Christians who lack the power of God live a life of defeat. Jesus did not die on the cross for us to live a defeated life. **Acts 1:8** says, *"But you will receive power when the Holy Spirit comes on you."* God gives us the power. Many Christians are not operating out of the power of the Holy Spirit. If we understand the resurrection, then we know things no longer have power over us. We have victory through Jesus' finished work on the cross.

As kingdom believers we are to seek ways to help advance God's eternal kingdom. God is tired of pretense in Christians. He doesn't want us Sunday after Sunday playing church; going with no desire to live a righteous life; He desires us to have a life that puts us in right relationship with Him. . In **Matthew 9:37** *Jesus told his disciples, "The harvest is plentiful but the workers are few."* God does not need any more secret service coward Christians. There are enough of them in the church. We have to take a stand for righteousness, *"Woe to those who call evil good, and good evil; Who put darkness for light, and light for darkness; Who put bitter for sweet, and sweet for bitter!"* **(Isaiah 5:20).**

The church has forsaken its relationship with God because we are committing spiritual adultery. We have now become lovers of other things (job, family, money, education, friends, men, women, etc.) until we have forgotten about our God. The Apostle Paul forewarned of spiritual adultery in **2 Timothy 3:1-5** when he said,
"But mark this: There will be terrible times in the last days. People will be lovers of themselves, lovers of money, boastful, proud, abusive, disobedient to their parents, ungrateful, unholy, without love, unforgiving, slanderous, without self-control, brutal, not lovers of the good, treacherous, rash, conceited, lovers of pleasure rather than lovers of God." We only remember God when the things we seek fail. God has become our side kick.

The ultimate goal of believers should be for God to equip us to minister in whatever burdens He has put before us. **2 Corinthians**

10: 15-18 says, *"Having hope as your faith is increased, we shall be greatly enlarged by you in our sphere, to preach the gospel in the regions beyond you, and not to boast in another man's sphere of accomplishment. But he who glories, let him glory in the Lord. For not he who commends himself is approved, but whom the Lord commends."* I challenge you as you read this book, seek to know your purpose in life, or you can choose to keep living like a sheep without a shepherd. **Matthew 9:36** says, *"When He saw the crowds, He had compassion for them, because they were harassed and helpless, like sheep without a shepherd."*

There are people who say God called them, but they are not walking in their assignment because there is no anointing on their lives. They could be preachers, teachers, singers, deacons, and trustees, etc. The Lord's rewards are a motivation for living a life of Christ-like character. What we believe about Jesus gets us to Heaven, but how we behave on behalf of Jesus determines our quality of Heavenly rewards. **James 1:12** says, *"Blessed is the man who remains steadfast under trial, for when he has stood the test he will receive the crown of life, which God has promised to those who love him."*

Our Father, who art in Heaven, I enter your gates with thanksgiving and your throne with praise. I ask that you speak to the person's heart reading this book in a mighty way. Give them a desire to seek your will and purpose for their life. Bless them to establish a lasting love affair with you, Lord, and experience the abiding of your shadow. Speak to them like you have never spoken before. Holy Spirit give them such a conviction to have a repenting heart crying out to you for forgiveness. Help them make the decision that the time has come to form an intimate relationship with you. I pray they do not walk in their emotions, but in the power and authority you have given them. I thank you God for working in them right now and it is done, in Jesus name. Amen.

TAKE COVER – WE ARE UNDER ATTACK
Chapter 2

When the trials come, and they come to all of us, we have the assurance that God will cover us under His wings as we seek refuge. Every born-again believer at one time or another will come under attack of the enemy. **Psalm 34:19** tells us, *"A righteous man may have many troubles, but the LORD delivers him from them all."* God gives us the assurance that He will deliver us.

The most powerful weapon against Satan is God's Holy Word. No power of darkness can stand against the Word of God. Thus, being rooted and grounded in the Word of God should not be an option for the believer. The biggest mistake many Christians make is they fail to have a personal relationship with God. They know of God, but they don't know God in a personal way. This can be compared to someone who runs out of gas. You know in advance your car needs gas, but you keep passing the gas stations. You eventually get gas once the car finally runs out.. Believers know the importance of the Word of God, but yet refuse to stop to pick up the Bible until an attack occurs.

The Bible tells us Satan comes to rob, steal and destroy, but God tells us He came for us to have life more abundantly. God wants us to live an abundant life, but we can only live in abundance if we are living in His shadow of righteousness. **Psalm 91:1** says, *"He who dwells in the secret place of the Most High Shall abide under the shadow of the Almighty."* We have to go through different types of attacks. Some attacks come directly from the enemy and some we bring upon ourselves because of our bad choices and actions. Nevertheless, God allows trials to come into our lives to build our character and so we can form our own personal relationship with Him. A personal relationship with

God causes us to desire to be more like Jesus in every aspect of our lives. So our lifestyle has to conform to the image of Jesus.

When the attack comes, in order for us to effectively fight and resist, we have to determine if it is a spiritual fight or our flesh we are fighting. When Job was being tested, he was in a spiritual battle. There was no sin or bad choices in his life which caused the attack. We know this because God initiated the test in **Job 1:8,** *"Then the LORD said to Satan, 'Have you considered my servant Job? There is no one on earth like him; he is blameless and upright, a man who fears God and shuns evil."* On the other hand, when the children of Israel were on the toughest battlefield of their nation's history, they were facing the most vicious enemy of all, themselves. They were attacked and experienced trials because of their rebellion and disobedience toward God.

Regardless of the source of the attack, spiritual or fleshly, there are three questions you must ask yourself to determine the kind of battle you are fighting. We must examine ourselves to see if we are in right relationship with God. If we are, then the battle is not ours, but it's the Lord's.
1. Am I living outside the will of God? (Sin)
2. Do I have any unconfessed sin? (Unforgiveness)
3. Is God simply working to complete me? (Destiny)

Am I Living Outside the Will of God? *"Ye cannot drink the cup of the Lord, and the cup of devils: ye cannot be partakers of the Lord's table, and of the table of devils"* **(1 Corinthians 10:21).**

God's will for us is to be formed in His image. We have to look, think, and act like Him. This doesn't happen overnight but this must be the goal of the believer. We must be committed to the process of taking on God's image. In doing so, we will take on His personality traits, which are love, joy, peace, patience, kindness, goodness, faithfulness, gentleness and self-control.

2) Do I have any unconfessed sin in my life? Sin can be described as an offense against God, such as deliberate rebellion, defiance, wickedness and ungodliness. We have to examine ourselves and ask, "Do any of these characteristics exist in me? Have I failed to forgive someone, or not asked for forgiveness from someone I may have offended? If the answer is yes, then you are walking in sin, which will definitely hinder your prayers. **Mark 11:25** says, *"And whenever you stand praying, if you have anything against anyone, forgive him, that your Father in Heaven may also forgive you your trespasses."* In addition to unforgiveness, there are other areas of sin, which we must identify and confess to God, such as fornication, homosexuality, lying, hypocrisy, and gossip. Sin separates us from God which makes us a prime target for attack. **Isaiah 59:2** says, *"But your iniquities have made a separation between you and your God, and your sins have hidden his face from you, so that He will not hear."*

3) Is God simply working to complete me? Some attacks, as in the case of Job, occur because either God initiated them or He is using the attacks to increase our spiritual maturity. Some attacks are not caused by sin, but simply not walking in the will of God. God wants to work spiritual completion and maturity in us. **Philippians 1:6** says, *"Being confident of this, that He who began a good work in you will carry it on to completion until the day of Christ Jesus."* These trials or attacks are not meant to hurt us, but to prosper us and bring about growth. When we are submitted to the authority of God, and when Satan comes in like a flood, the spirit of the Lord will lift up a standard against him. Because Job was submitted to the authority of God, the standard was lifted when God told Satan not to put a hand on Job. That statement proves the devil has limited power over the children of God. Though Job suffered and lost all of his earthly possessions, in the end, the Lord rewarded Job double for his trouble.

To abide under the shadow is not merely quoting scriptures, attending church, singing on the choir, or doing church activities. These works will not keep us or bring about deliverance during the times of trouble. However, through our obedience, yielding to God's authority, and the power of the Holy Spirit, we are able to defeat the enemy in our lives. As we submit to Christ's authority, we will be in consistent authority over the enemy. Our heart must become a transformed vessel to God and His word.

- Yes, you may be going through an attack and you may want to quit, but don't give up!
- Believe no weapon formed against you will prosper.
- Do not be overcome by adversity (hardship, difficulty, hard times, misfortune, and danger) continue to dwell in that secret place.
- Stop running away from your problems by becoming depressed, turning to alcohol, drugs, or overeating, etc. Instead run into the arms of God and His Word.
- Live with the power of God to win. That same resurrection power that raised Jesus from the dead lives in us and because of that, the battle has already been won.

Psalm 57:1

Be gracious to me, O God, be gracious to me, For my soul takes refuge in You; And in the shadow of Your wings I will take refuge until destruction passes by.

DON'T BE CONSUMED BY THE STORM
SPIRITUAL STORMS
Chapter 3

I am confident as I write, I am at a time in my life where God told Satan that I belong to God and He has me in training. He is teaching me how to walk in His shadow. Just as God initiated the test for Job, I know He has done the same for me to build my character. God set me up with this storm for a faith test.

Many of you are being set up for God's divine purpose. Perhaps you are going through the toughest trial and darkest point of your life. Remember Jesus is praying for us, just like He did for Peter, that our faith does not fail us. In Luke 22:32, Jesus said, *"But I have prayed for you, Simon, that your faith may not fail. And when you have turned back, strengthen your brothers."*

Maybe you have lost a child, a loved one, or a job that concerns you. Maybe your challenge is a financial struggle or legal battle. Perhaps it's a divorce, terminal illness, addiction, or even suicidal thoughts and depression attacking you. Regardless of how you feel at this moment, God is saying, *"Don't give up I will rescue you."* Remember Jesus is praying for you.

This is NOT the time for our trust, faith, and hope in God to waiver. We have to keep our eyes focused on God, not the storm. Jesus is looking to see your eyes, don't disappoint Him. Look at Him and try not to blink because any distraction, however slight, will cause you to sink. Be mindful of the people you surround yourself with when going through a trial. Don't listen or vent to anyone who is not speaking God's word, because God says **John 6:63,** *"The words I* *speak, they are spirit and life."* Any other words will cause us to lose focus and you cannot afford to be distracted.

The tides of the storm are raging, but we have to stay on the ship. God's children have been given a life jacket made up of His divine sustaining power. You and I will make it to the other side if we just hold on a little longer. It may even look like he is winning, but remember things are not what they appear to be. Use your spiritual lens and the eyes of faith to believe that God has won us the victory. God won the battle on Calvary's Cross and confirmed this when Jesus said, *"It is finished,"* (**John 19:30**).

Perhaps you cannot eat or sleep, but this is only for a short while because know that weeping only lasts for a night, but joy comes in the morning. In any storm, fear may rise up and try to defeat us. If fear has already reared its ugly head in your life, just know God has not given you a spirit of fear, but of power, love and a sound mind. Fear is only a trick of the enemy. When it comes, do not be caught off guard for it's only a trick. We don't walk in fear, but faith.

Staying in the shadow of God is especially important while in a storm. It is only in God's shadow you will be protected and come out victoriously. You can remain in God's shadow by communing with God through prayer, fasting, reading the Bible, and spending time with Him. Your relationship with God has to go beyond the surface level, you must engage in true intimacy with Him.

Remember this is just a test and our Father is training us how to walk in His shadow. Even if we somehow brought the trials on ourselves through sin or bad judgment, God still uses the trials to train and teach us. The Lord will never leave nor forsake us. He promised He will be with us until the end of the world. Believe me, there is victory in the storm. If we remain steadfast with God, we will come out stronger.

Storms can make us bitter or better. The choice is yours to make! Be assured we will only become stronger and more spiritually mature if we remain in God's shadow and in His presence throughout the storm. At the end, our test will become our testimony. We will be able to share what the enemy tried to use for our harm. **Romans 8:28** says, *"…And we know all things work together for the good of those who love God, and those who are the called according to His purpose.*

One Saturday morning, I needed to go to the post office to meet a mailing deadline. I was home alone, so I had to take my baby daughter out with me. It was a very windy morning and when I got outside the wind was so strong, it literally took my child's breath away. I immediately wrapped my jacket over her little face to shield her from the wind. The Holy Spirit whispered in my ears, *"That's how I shield you from the storms in your life."* God reassured me all was well.

What proof would we have that we have gone through the storm trusting God? When we can walk uprightly in the midst of the test, with our head held high, like a proud soldier, equipped with the full armor of God. We know we are covered by the shadow of Almighty God because we have been washed in the blood of the lamb. We are reminded that Jesus walked on the water and calmed the sea and He will calm our storms as well. Calming the seas of life's storms is God's character.

Second, we can praise God in the test with a smile on our face, a prayer of thanksgiving, and a heart filled with praise. We have the blessed assurance in knowing that *God can do exceedingly and abundantly above all you can think or ask according to the power that works in us* **(Ephesians 3:20).** We are now walking by faith and not by sight. We have replaced fear with faith because we can't have faith and walk in fear at the same time. Faith is what God is developing in us. Once we reach this point, we have lost sight of the storm and can only see our Father's face. The test is almost done and the raging storm is ceasing. Let the joy of the Lord be our strength as we cross the finish line. Then we are commissioned to reach back, once we get to other side, and help someone else to do the same. Luke 22:32 says, "But I have prayed for you, Simon, that your faith may not fail. And when you have turned back, strengthen your brothers.

Third, as we walk through the valley of the shadow of death, we will fear no evil because our Father is right there with us. The Sunday morning my mom went home with God we recited Psalm chapter 23 in unison before she left us. After we finished, she said, "I have good peace." What she was telling us was that she was covered under the shadow of God and she had no fear of dying. Most importantly, in God's shadow there is a peace that surrounds us that can only come from God. This is the peace that will bring you to the shore as long as your mind stays on God. (Isaiah 26:3).

Father, God, don't let my emotions consume me. Sometimes the way feels dark because of my grief and pain. God, but let my faith in you be so much greater than my emotions. Sometimes I don't see my circumstances changing, but let me know that you are working in the spirit realm on by behalf. Lord let me be reminded that faith is not based on what I see, but rather the divine finished work you performed on the cross for me.

Lord I ask that you trade my ashes for your crown beauty. Trade my mourning and grief for the oil of joy. Finally, trade my despair for a garment of praise. Lord I pray to get into your presence where these exchanges take place. For your word says in your presence is the fullness of joy.

I choose to give you thanks today and believe that this season of darkness is already gone. Thank you that you have promised you will never leave nor forsake me. I thank you and praise you, by faith it is done in the matchless name of Jesus. Amen.

PERSONAL TESTIMONY ON WAITING ON THE LORD
Chapter 4

I had to wait on the Lord as my faith was tested throughout a legal storm my family and I had to endure. I now know that if I were not rooted in the Word of God, I would have lost my mind. There were times when I felt like giving up, but I waited on the Lord because I knew He would renew my strength. Through this storm, God was preparing me for ministry. I knew in order to survive I had to begin and maintain a strict spiritual diet in the Word of God. I had to:

- Meditate on God's word day and night.
- I ate the word of God, "Then He said to me, "Son of man, eat this scroll I am giving you and fill your stomach with it." So I ate it, and it tasted as sweet as honey in my mouth (**Ezekiel 3:3**).
- I hid God's word in my heart because in the heart is where God searches our intent, *"For the LORD searches all hearts, and understands every intent of the thoughts If you seek Him, He will let you find Him; but if you forsake Him, He will reject you forever,"* (**1 Chronicles 28: 9b**).
- I had to persevere and say like the servant Job, *"If a man dies, will he live again? All the days of my struggle I will wait until my change comes,"* (**Job 14:14**).

WALKING TO THE BEAT OF A DIFFERENT DRUMMER
Chapter 5

God spoke to me in prayer and said that He is looking for believers that He can use in these last days. He is looking for His children who are in the world, but not of the world. In other words, He is looking for the ones who will be willing to walk to the beat of a different drummer, and that drummer is God Almighty. We cannot walk with God if we have not been born again.

Nicodemus asked if he had to enter his mother's womb to be born again (John 3). No, to be saved, you have to repent of your sins, turn from your wicked sinful nature, and believe in your heart that Christ died on the cross and has risen from the dead. If you have not accepted Jesus into your heart as your personal Savior, please do so now by simply repeating this prayer:

> *Lord Jesus, I admit that I am a sinner. Forgive me of my sins. I confess with my mouth the Lord Jesus and believe in my heart that Jesus died, and was raised from the dead. I invite you into my heart to help me to live a life that pleases you.*
> *Amen.*

Have you got the beat? You can only walk with God if you are His child, because God walks a path of righteousness and you have to be saved to walk this path. There are so many people in the church who are not saved but think that they are. *Everyone who says Lord, Lord, will not enter in the kingdom, God will say," Get away from me, I do not know you."* **(Matthew 7:21, 23)**. Many church goers are working in the church believing that the works will bring about salvation, but it is not in the works. Our works do not save us; we work because we are saved through the grace of God.

Members of the body of Christ are not to be conformed to this world's standards. God can only use those who are available, and that are in right relationship with Him. He is able to use those who possess the love of God. He created us in His image, wanting to shape His children's character that they might be more like him. God wants us to cultivate the fruit of the spirit which includes *love, joy, peace, longsuffering, gentleness, goodness, faith meekness, temperance* **(Galatians 5:22)**. We can attain the attributes of this fruit only through spending time with God, studying, and applying His word. *Jesus said, "I am the true vine, and my Father is the husbandman. Every branch in me beareth not fruit he taketh away: and every branch that beareth fruit, he purgeth it, that it may bring forth more fruit."* **(John 15:1-2)**. This scripture tells us that there are many who confess to being Christians but they are bearing no fruit. When we see a vine we look to see what kind of fruit it is bearing. Therefore, if we are the branches connected to the Vine, we should bear fruit. When we confess to be a Christian we should see Christ-like behavior displayed in our lives. If not, maybe we were never connected to the Vine by faith. *If a man remains in me and I in him, he will bear much fruit; apart from me you can do nothing."*

Without faith we cannot please God. Through faith we accepted salvation and the promises of God's word. Only through faith can we gain access to Christ. Walking in God's shadow requires a child-like faith, because we know that the just person lives by faith. If we fail to be obedient to God due to our sinful nature because we want to satisfy our flesh, we will encounter a separation from God. This separation severs our relationship until we get back in right standing with God.

I believe that we must be sold on the fruit of love. *Jesus replied, "Thou shalt love the Lord your God with all your heart and with all your soul and with all your mind."* This is the first and greatest commandment. And the second is like unto it, *"Thou shalt love thy neighbor as thyself. On these commandments hang all the law."* **(Matthew 22:36-40).** There is not enough love among the body of Christ. Therefore, that is one of the main reasons we do not see miracles taking place and the greater works that Jesus said we would be able to perform. The church lacks spiritual strength because the power and presence of God is not at work, due to our disobedience to God's word. Little faith is practice and very little Godly love is being shown for each other. God's ultimate desire is for us to love others the way He loves us. Our loving Father has set the example for us to follow, and until we display this love we will not be able to walk in the promised abundant life. We have to decide if we are walking to the beat of the world or the beat from Heaven.

PEACE IN THE STORM
Chapter 6

At first glance, the subject of peace seems strange or odd when we think of the spiritual warfare. How can one be at peace when he or she is in a storm? Well, we have to understand that peace is a spiritual weapon that Jesus has already given us. Jesus said in **John 14:27**, *"Peace I leave with you; my peace I give you. I do not give to you as the world gives. Do not let your hearts be troubled and do not be afraid."*

> PEACE HAS ALREADY BEEN ESTABLISHED FOR US. WE DO NOT HAVE TO PRAY FOR IT. LOOK AT PEACE SIMILAR TO THAT OF A CARPENTER WHO BUILDS A HOUSE FOR YOU AND SAYS IT IS FINISHED, ALL YOU HAVE TO DO IS TAKE OWNERSHIP. JESUS SAID ON THE CROSS, "IT IS FINISHED!" (JOHN 19:30).
> TAKE OWNERSHIP OF YOUR PEACE.

Peace has already been established for us; we do not have to pray for it. Take ownership of your peace.
We have to learn and understand through the Word of God how to take possession of our peace.

> *Oh Lord, give me revelation knowledge and spiritual wisdom to understand that it is finished, because I believe that you have already given me peace!" In Jesus Name, Amen.*

When we understand that Jesus is the way by which we have obtained peace, we can go through life battles knowing the battle is not ours, it is the Lord's. However, there is an enemy on the loose whose assignment is to steal, kill, and destroy, (**John 10:10**) and he comes to take our peace and torment us. If we are not operating in the Kingdom principles found in the word of God, we will never be able to find that place of peace in our trials. Once we lose our peace in any situation we have lost the battle. Without peace we cannot hear God. Some symptoms of having no peace are fearful, faint-hearted, panicking, trembling, despair, doubt, anxious, and restless. God knew that one of the enemy's greatest weapon is putting fear in our mind. It is no coincidence that the phrase "fear not" or "be not afraid" appears in the bible 365 times. One of my favorite verses in the Bible is *"Fear not, for I am with you; be not dismayed, for I am God; I will strengthen you, I will help you, I will uphold you with my righteous right hand"* **(Isaiah 41:10).**

Walking in peace comes when we practice the things we know to be true, which are the promises in the Word of God. **Isaiah 26:3** tells us, *"Thou wilt keep him in perfect peace, whose mind is stayed on thee; because he trusteth in thee."* It is a fight to keep our mind on God. Yes, you heard me say fight because it is a struggle to focus on God when we are going through a trial. It is a struggle because the evil one is fighting so hard to get us to lose our focus on God so that the storm can consume us. If we do not persevere to keep our focus on God, the enemy will win. Say to yourself and believe that you are victorious, *"because the Spirit who lives in me is greater than the spirit who lives in the world"* **(1 John 4:4).**

How do we know when we are walking in peace? Peace comes when we surrender to God's will. We surrender by refusing to allow our hearts and minds to entertain thoughts which fall short of truth and righteousness. We have to study God's Word which is the truth that sets us free from the bondage of this world. The Apostle Paul instructs us to have our feet shod with the preparation of the gospel of peace (**Ephesians 6:15)**. What does that mean? The word shod means spiritual shoes. A person walking in peace has to put on their spiritual shoes. In the spirit they are able to walk by faith, not by sight (**2 Corinthians 5:7**). A person walking in peace has allowed his footsteps to be ordered by the Lord, because in peace you can hear God. A person living in peace, lives by faith, walks by faith, and refuses to live in fear!

When you lose your peace, you become helpless because you are under the control of the evil one. You have surrendered your authority and power that God has given you. You become so focused on the problem that you lose sight of God, the problem solver. Finally, I know what it is to lose your peace and be tormented by the enemy. I lost my peace because I was trying to fight a spiritual battle with natural weapons. I had to receive a revelation that I was not wrestling against flesh and blood, but against principalities, against powers, against the ruler of darkness, and against spiritual wickedness in high places (**Ephesians 6:12)**. The Bible says in **John 8:32,** *"You shall know the truth, and the truth shall make you free."* There were truths I had to reconcile in my walk so I could take back my peace. I got back in right standing with God. I started walking in the rights and privileges, the blessings of God, and His protection He granted.

I had to acknowledge my position in Christ. Do you know your position in Christ Jesus? Our position now is that we are united, joint heirs, with Christ. Psalm 107:2 says, *"Let the redeemed of the Lord say so, Whom He has redeemed from the hand of the enemy."* We are the redeemed bought with a price. We no longer walk under the influence of the enemy. As a believer, to know your position, privileges, and the protection of God is vital to your life. Grace be to God, when I found out that I needed the divine weapons that can only come from God to defeat the enemy, that battle was over. We need the supernatural power of God at work in our lives because we cannot fight the devil nor endure our trials with our natural abilities or intellect.

I challenge you to make the decision to walk in the peace of God. You and only you have to get fed up with walking your Christian walk with no peace and no power. I pray that God will strengthen your inner man and I challenge you to rise up in the spirit realm, take your position of victory, walk in the privileges and promises of God and His protection. **Psalm 91:14-16** says, *"Because he has focused his love on me, I will deliver him. I will protect him because he knows my name. He shall call upon me, and I will answer him: I will be with him in trouble; I will deliver him, and honour him. With long life will I satisfy him and show him my salvation."*

Nothing is more disturbing than to observe a believer who has lost his peace. We can have the peace of God that is taught in the Bible. We cannot fight a spiritual war without peace, because peace is a part of our spiritual armor. Love God. Know Him for yourself, and have confidence that He will answer you when you pray according to His divine will. Put on your spiritual shoes and keep walking in the peace of God.

WORSHIP GOD WHILE GOING THROUGH THE STORM
Worship = The Worth Of God!
Chapter 7

With a natural storm, we get warnings. Meteorologists watch and give updates on the weather as they approach. Unfortunately, most spiritual storms come upon us suddenly. Spiritual storms have a God-driven purpose. Storms allow us to see the goodness of the Lord. Most times, experiencing God's goodness pushes us into our purpose. While God does not send all storms, He uses the storms for purpose, **Jeremiah 29:11-12** says, *"For I know the plans I have for you, declares the LORD, plans to prosper you and not to harm you, plans to give you hope and a future. Then you will call upon Me and go and pray to Me, and I will listen to you."* Many believers emphasize Jeremiah 29:11 but fail to read verse 12. Prayer is the one most powerful weapon for believers. Prayer enables us to keep our connection to our power source, which is our loving God. We must pray and thank God for His goodness and His sovereignty. We are commanded to give thanks in all things, even the storms.

God created us to enter into a relationship with Him. It is through relationship, that worship takes place. True worship cannot take place outside of a relationship with God! We must learn how to worship God as we go through our storms of life. Worship takes our mind off problems and circumstances and allow us to put our focus back on God. The more God- focused we are, the smaller the problem will appear because we have shifted our eyes from the problem to the problem solver.

Worship means the worth of God. What is God worth to you? We don't worship God for what He can give us, we worship Him for what He has already done for us. **John 3:16** reminds us of God's ultimate sacrifice for us. It says, *"For God so loved the world that He gave his one and only Son, that whoever believes in him shall not perish but have eternal life."*

Worship takes place in our hearts which is part of our spirit. True worship can only happen in the presence of God. One characteristic of God is that He is holy. Leviticus 10:3 says, *"By those who come near Me I must be regarded as holy; and before all the people I must be glorified."* When we acknowledge and recognize the holiness of God, we can't help but worship Him. Worship takes us into the presence of God and praise is what we do when we get into God's presence.

When Jesus encountered the Samaritan woman at the well He explained true worship. Jesus taught this woman that true worshippers can only worship God in spirit and truth because God is spirit. He went on to say that the Father is seeking true worshippers to worship Him. Unfortunately, many of our churches are not teaching their parishioners what Jesus taught the Samaritan woman. Therefore, they cannot do what they do not know. Some believers think, and are indeed trying to worship God in a natural or physical way, but we can only come into God's presence in the spirit realm. Furthermore, **1 Corinthians 2:14** states, *"But the natural man does not receive the things of the Spirit of God, for they are foolishness to him; nor can he know them, because they are spiritually discerned."*

Rest assured that our storms do not take God by surprise. He knows when we are going through a storm. Realistically, because we are going through our storm, we do not have to wait for the storm to end to worship God. We praise God because we are fully persuaded that we will go through to the other side. If we could take hold of true worship, prior to our spiritual storms, it would make worship an easier reality while in the storm. However, worshipping God during a storm will not take us out of it, but it will help us endure it.

Psalm 150:6 says, *"Let everything that has breath praise the LORD. Praise ye the LORD."* The amazing thing about this is God can use the wrath of men to praise Him. God used Pharaoh's stubbornness and rebellion so that His name would be praised. **Romans 9:17** says, *"As recorded in scripture as saying to Pharaoh: I raised you up for this very purpose, that I might display my power in you and that my name might be proclaimed in all the earth."*

Let's view how King David modeled true worship. The scriptures tell us that David laid aside his royal robes and appeared in the distinctive dress of a priest. The Bible said David danced before the LORD with all his might. King David worshipped God by dancing before Him.

When we go through storms, like David, we must learn how to take off our most adored worldly apparel. Things will get in our way of true worship. In true worship nothing matters but the worth of God and who He is to you. Despite what you might be going through, learn how to worship the true and living God.

Paul and Silas were arrested in Philippi for casting a demon out of a slave girl. The demon was an affliction upon the girl, but it was profit for the slaveholders. This slave girl earned a great deal of money for her owners by fortune-telling. The Romans saw Paul and Silas as a threat to their power and money. Therefore, Paul and Silas were arrested, beaten, and thrown into prison because of their faith and stance for God. During their circumstance, Paul and Silas were still able to worship God. There are many who might have thrown themselves a pity party, but Paul and Silas chose to throw themselves a prayer party. They did not wait until they were out of their storm to worship God, they worshipped in the midst of the storm. They worshipped through praying and singing hymns to God. In the prison, I can imagine them saying, "*I will bless the Lord at all times: his praise shall continually be in my mouth. My soul shall make her boast in the Lord: the humble shall hear thereof and be glad. O magnify the Lord with me and let us exalt his name together."* (**Psalm 34:1-3**).

Supernaturally, there was an earthquake and the gates of the jail swung open because they worshipped God (**Acts 16:25-26**). It is so important that we learn how to worship and praise God, because it is vital when we are going through our trials. Our storms can be used to put us on our destiny track. We see in the Bible when Joseph's brother sold him into slavery to the Midianites, (**Genesis 37:28**) Joseph went from the pit, to Potiphar's house, and prison before he got to his destiny. God used Joseph's brothers' cruel act to promote him as second ruler over Egypt.

The thief comes only to steal, kill, and destroy us; however the enemy has been defeated. Jesus disarmed the powers of the enemy on the cross. Do you want to live the abundant life? Learn how to worship God in your storm! He will never leave nor forsake us, but will be right in the midst of the storm with us.

WAITING ON THE LORD IN THE MIDST OF THE STORM
Chapter 8

If you were to take a survey of Christians, you will find that most will tell you that they are waiting on the Lord to do something in their lives. They are praying for God to get them out of a spiritual storm or help them to endure the one they're in. Well, there is nothing wrong with that, for most who are waiting on the Lord are going through some kind of trial, tribulation, sickness, suffering, etc. Christians struggle with disappointments and suffering in their lives. We know this because Jesus made it clear that in this world we will have trouble. However we get encouraging words from **John 16:33** where Jesus says, *"But take heart! I have overcome the world."* Jesus will help you overcome so rejoice because victory has been won.

The Bible says in **Psalm 34:19**, *"Many are the afflictions of the righteous: but the LORD delivereth him out of them all."* So it's justifiable that we wait on God because He is the only one who can change our heart, our situation, and help us endure our trials.

However, I have come to realize one thing: some have yet to understand that while we are waiting for God, He is usually waiting on us to do something. One of God's characteristics is patience. He waits on us to repent. **2 Peter 3:9** says, *"The Lord is not slack concerning his promise, as some men count slackness; but is longsuffering to us-ward, not willing that any should perish, but that all should come to repentance."*

There is a God side and a man side that must be executed. This may be one of the reasons we wait longer than we need to. We've got to do our part in the midst of a storm. Until then, we may never realize the revelation of God's plan for our individual lives.

> **WHAT WE DO WHILE WE WAIT MAY DETERMINE THE OUTCOME OF OUR WAITING.**

Secondly, God is not going to do what He has empowered us to do for ourselves. Finally, I believe some trials we bring upon ourselves, therefore they are punitive, which means it will be used as a corrective measure. So the question now becomes what is God waiting on us to do? Many times, God is waiting on us to turn to righteous living by aligning our life with His divine plan. In order to move to righteous living, our ultimate goal has to be to get in line with God's will for our lives. We can do this through establishing a deeper, more intimate relationship with Him. This relationship can be created by spending time with God through prayer, studying the Bible, and worship. We are to examine ourselves daily in an effort to reconcile ourselves to God's Holy will. One of my favorite scriptures regarding my examination of faith can be found in **2 Corinthians 13:5**, *"Examine yourselves to see whether you are in the faith; test yourselves. Do you not realize that Christ Jesus is in you-unless, of course, you fail the test?"*

What we do while we wait may determine the outcome of our waiting. What are you doing while you wait? In the midst of our storms we will need our spiritual strength renewed. Only through God can our inner man be strengthened. Some may be familiar with the song, "I Don't Mind Waiting," but truthfully, waiting on God is not always comfortable. There are three virtues I suggest you consider that will help you persevere through your storm.

1. **Spiritual Diet** - The diet must consist of the Word of God. Eat

it day and night. The Bible tells us to spend time in the word of God to show ourselves approved unto God, a workman needeth not to be ashamed by rightly dividing the word of truth (**2 Timothy 2:15**). Let the word dwell richly in you by meditating on it day and night and God will give us good success (**Psalm 1:1-3**). We need to hide God's words in our heart. David said , *"I have hidden your word in my heart, that I might not sin against thee,"* (**Psalm 119:11**). We will need God's word to guide us by being a lamp unto our feet, and a light unto our path (**Psalm 119:105**). God spoke the earth into existence. We should acknowledge that the power that made the world exist is working in us every day to conform us to the image of God. Therefore, we have to speak life into dead situations by using the word of God. In **John 6:63**, Jesus said, *"The Spirit gives life; the flesh counts for nothing. The words I have spoken to you are spirit and life."*

2. Spiritual Exercise – There are some things we have to exercise for the Holy Spirit to develop our character while we wait on the manifestation to prayer. We exercise the word of God while on our spiritual diet. We must exercise these qualities:

- **Love** – Do you love God? *"Love the Lord your God with all your heart and with all your soul and with all your mind and with all your strength. And the second is like, namely this, Thou shalt love thy neighbour as thyself. There is none other commandment greater than these,"* (**Mark 12:30-31**). Are we seeking His face or His hand? Love is not looking for what we can get from God. We should be asking God what we can do to help expand the Kingdom. We must also love others. Do you love your brother? *"By this all will know that you are My disciples, if you have love for one another,"* (**John 13:35**).

- **Forgiveness-** Have you forgiven everyone that has hurt or offended you? Have you gone and ask forgiveness from the person you hurt or offended? Ask yourself, is there anyone I need to forgive or anyone I need to ask to forgive me?

- **Prayer** - Waiting in silence, listening to hear from God is key in the waiting process. While David waited in silence to hear from God he declared, *"My soul waits in silence for God only; from Him is my* *salvation.... My soul wait in silence for God only, for my hope is from Him,"* **(Psalm 62:1, and 5,)**. How is your prayer life? Keep your communication line open because the Bible tells us that men ought to always pray. In our prayers as we examine ourselves God will show us the things in our lives that are not like Him. *"Knowing that the effectual fervent prayer of the righteous availeth much,"* **(James 5:16ᵇ)**.

- **Faith** – Spend more time reading and listening to the Word of God because faith comes by hearing the Word of God. You will need faith because without faith it is impossible to please Him, for he that cometh to Him must believe that He exists and that He will reward them who diligently seek him **(Hebrews 11:6)**.

- **Joy** – Do you have joy? Are you cheerful in conversation? Is your delight in the Lord? The joy of the Lord has to become your strength. As you endure the storm, you must do so with a joyful heart. Notice, I didn't say *"happiness"* because happiness is dependent on external circumstances. Joy is dependent upon your relationship with God. *"The Lord is my strength and shield. I trust him with all my heart. He helps me, and my heart is filled with joy. I burst out in songs of thanksgiving,"* (P**salm 28:7**). It is possible to maintain your joy in a storm because God is with you and His presence is the basis of your joy!

- **Peace-** *"Thou will keep him in perfect peace whose mind is stayed on thee because he trusteth in thee,"* **(Isaiah 26:3)**. Are you at peace with God? If you are not at peace with Him, you cannot be at peace with others in your life. Peace is not the absence of problems. Instead, it's having a calmness in your spirit because you know that God is in control and He always leads you to victory!

- **Patience** – Do you have the patience to wait on God? Do not complain to others, but pour out your complaints before God and never make any complaints against Him? Remember that we are not to be anxious for anything, but in prayer and supplication, with thanksgiving, make our requests known before God **(Philippians 4:6)**. Being easily frustrated and irritable while in a storm is a primary indication that you are not walking in patience.

- **Rest in the Spirit**– How can we rest in God in the midst of a storm? Read and meditate on scriptures; pray and ask God to give you a revelation to restore your peace. Peace precedes rest. Rest and wait patiently for him (**Psalm 37:7**). God rested on the seventh day after creating the earth, not because He was tired, but because He was finished. When we have done all we can do just stand in the victory of the cross and take your position of rest!

REJOICE IN THE LORD
Chapter 9

"Rejoice in the Lord always: and again I say Rejoice," (**Philippians 4:4, NIV**). The Apostle Paul was in prison when he wrote this letter to the Philippians. He used the words joy and rejoice at least 16 times in this short letter. This letter was written to define and describe the attribute of joy. One main purpose of Paul was to encourage the Philippians to stand firm in the face of persecution and rejoice regardless of their circumstances. Today, I agree with Paul in saying we must learn how to rejoice in the midst of our trials because we are in a spiritual war. Rejoicing not for the trials, but we rejoice knowing the battle has been won. Hallelujah!

Jesus said in **John 16:33** *"I have told you these things, so that in Me you may have peace. In this world you will have trouble. But take heart! I have overcome the world."* Jesus knew that there is an enemy in this world and the culture we live in would be evil. He knew in the midst of our troubles, trials and persecution, we would have to find a place of peace where we could find some joy.

Philippians 4:4 is a commandment that is repeated twice for emphasis. The joy that Paul talks about does not come from circumstances, but from the Holy Spirit who gives the believers a confidence of God's presence no matter what happens. This joy in the Lord which we must aim for is not a superficial happiness based on circumstances or even on the absence of trials. Rather, it's a solid, abiding contentment, and hope that is as steady and certain as our faithful God.

To rejoice in the Lord always does not mean that we will never feel depressed or sad. It's okay to feel sad at times because sadness is an emotion that God put in us. However, we should not allow ourselves to fall into a *"spirit"* of sadness or depression. This joy is an attitude of hope and contentment that rises above circumstances and focuses on the very character of God. That's why Paul could say in **Philippians 4:11**, *"I am not saying this because I am in need, for I have learned to be content in any circumstance."*

1. To rejoice in the Lord always is an attitude which depends on our choice.
2. To rejoice in the Lord always is not a matter of feeling, but of our obedience.
3. To rejoice in the Lord always is a command that we must deliberately choose to obey, especially when we're in difficult circumstances.

So, when we go through trials, when we're treated unfairly, when we're disappointed by people or circumstances, we are faced with a decision. Now the question becomes will I obey this command to rejoice in the Lord or will I allow myself to be swept along by my feelings?

We find that Paul and Silas (**Acts 16:22-23**) were arrested, beaten and thrown into prison because of their faith and stance for God, they had all opportunity to become bitter or caught up in their feelings. Yet, they were still able to rejoice in the Lord. Many of us would have thrown a pity party, but Paul and Silas chose to throw a *prayer party*. They did not wait until they were out of their situation to worship God, they worshipped in the midst of the storm. They worshipped through praying and singing hymns to God while in the prison, I can imagine them saying, *"I will bless the Lord at all times: His praise shall continually be in my mouth. My soul shall make her boast in the Lord: the humble shall hear thereof, and be glad. O magnify the Lord with me, and let us exalt his name together."* (**Psalm 34:1-3**).

God intends for every believer to know and experience this same joy in the Lord, especially in difficult times. Joy is a fruit of the Holy Spirit. It is so important that we learn how to worship, praise, and rejoice in the time of trouble because it is vital for our survival.

When Paul wrote the letter encouraging the Philippians to learn how to rejoice in hard times, he knew what the outcome would be if they did not. **Nehemiah 8:10** says, *"Do not sorrow, for the joy of the LORD is your strength."*

If you don't find a place of joy, you may become depressed. If you are constantly depressed and weighed down with cares of the world, you're not an attractive role model for the Kingdom of God.

We can't be effective leaders in the church, or godly examples to our families if we are dominated by depression. Many believers sit in church Sunday after Sunday because they're trying to get the effects of the "goose bump feeling" of worship. That goose bump feeling will never carry you in any experience you may be having. Worshipping God is an exchange. He reveals His secrets as you give Him your absolute. Admitting that you're nothing and He's everything. We can ONLY worship God in the spirit and in the truth. That is the REAL secret to worship.

The Bible is very clear that the spirit of heaviness is connected to depression. Therefore, depression is a spirit that leads to a disconnection from God. If we are not careful, depression can open the door to what the Bible calls a python spirit.

You can find this spirit in (Acts 16:16-18) when Paul encounters a girl possessed with a spirit of divination. The word divination in this verse means python. That's why many call this evil force the python spirit.

When we think of a python snake, we know pythons are some of the largest snakes. To kill their prey they use an ambush technique where they grab their prey with their teeth before squeezing it to death.

A disconnect from God can sometimes allow a python spirit to come upon us. Similar to that of the python snake, the python spirit can put a chokehold on the believers' mind, health, finances, etc. The python spirit in the Bible is a winding spirit that works to squeeze out the breath of life (the Holy Spirit) and cut off your lifeline to God (prayer life). Also, the python spirit comes with a spirit of lies and deceptions. It will remind you of wounds from your past, surround you with demonic influences that tempt you to compromise the Word of God—or just bombard you with circumstances that will knock the wind out of you. That's why Psalm 27:13 says, *"I would have fainted had I not believed that I would see the goodness of the LORD in the land of the living."*

There are many symptoms of a python spirit attack that may include weariness, a loss of passion to worship and pray, feeling pressured, overwhelmed, helpless and even hopeless. The severity of these symptoms depends on how long this enemy has been coiling itself around you or your mind, and how much pressure it has applied. The python spirit will attack when we let our guard down or when we stop praying and spending time with God. It can keep you in bed to the point where you can't even lift your head. It can attack anyone, even our children. This spirit can cause a person to want or commit suicide. We must recognize the early warning signs of an attack and recognize ways you may have unknowingly given it access into your home and your life. This spirit can be passed down to our children and grandchildren if it is not rebuked or freed. Please don't be dismayed because there is victory in Jesus. Greater is He that is in us than he that is in the world. The word of God tells us that "Behold, I give unto you power to tread on serpents and scorpions, and over all the power of the enemy: and nothing shall by any means hurt you

(Luke 10:19). With Jesus we win! Jesus came so that we could live the abundant life.

DESTINED TO WALK IN THE SPIRIT
Chapter 10

Now that we have comprehended the purpose of our trials and tribulations, we must realize that it was all done to prepare us to walk in the Spirit. We hear a lot about walking in the supernatural or Spirit, but what does it mean to walk in the Spirit? This is a question that many of us do not fully understand. The presence of God is walking in His shadow which is His spirit. Walking in the Spirit happens when we walk in God's shadow of righteousness. Psalm 91:1 says, *"He that dwelleth in the secret place of the most High shall abide under the shadow of the Almighty."* God is righteous. A person walking in the Spirit under God's shadow has to walk in the Spirit of God.

In order to walk in the Spirit, we have to acquire a revelation from God. Revelation knowledge comes through us hearing and studying the Word or God. The Word is quickened in our born-again spirit where it moves from information or facts to transformation in our hearts. The word in our spirit becomes alive and it has power, and it gives us the ability to walk in the Spirit, also referred to as the supernatural.

We can't walk in the Spirit until our mind has been transformed, don't copy the behavior and customs of this world, but let God transform you into a new person by changing the way you think. Then you will learn to know God's will for you, which is good and pleasing and perfect (**Romans 12:2 NLT**). The scripture tells us that God has dealt each of us a measure of faith (**Romans 12:3**) and as a result of our trials and struggles our faith is activated thereby aiding us to walk in the supernatural.

In **Genesis 1:26,** God said, *"Let us make mankind in our image, in our likeness, so that they may rule over the fish in the sea and the birds in the sky, over the livestock and all the wild animals, and over all the creatures that move along the ground."* That verse explains the dominion God gave the believer. The Bible tells us that God created us in both spirit and flesh, but spirit first. God is a supernatural being with supernatural power. God is our creator and role model. We were created to move in the power of God, in the supernatural, or what we refer to as the Spirit realm.

During our faith walk with God, we discover how to walk in the Spirit and experience the same power the New Testament church possessed. The disciples in the New Testament walked in the power of the Holy Spirit. Jesus told his disciples, that they would receive power when the Holy Spirit comes on them; and they would be His witnesses in Jerusalem, and in all Judea and Samaria, and to the ends of the earth (**Acts 1:8**). As disciples, we cannot activate that power except through the supernatural which is the Spirit realm.

There are two Domains – the natural and supernatural: 1) Natural is composed of matter, time, and space; our senses what we can touch, see, taste or smell; things that are visible. 2) Supernatural is composed of the invisible, eternal and it never changes. Supernatural has dominion over the natural. The supernatural is faith at work. One might ask, why do we need the supernatural? Well, I will offer four reasons we need the supernatural:

1) We need the supernatural in order for miracles to take place. There are 28 chapters in the book of Acts and in every chapter, you find miracles taking place. One reason why young people don't want to come to church is because they see more power in the lights in the night clubs, then they see in the church. People are sleeping in church pews because services have become so boring, and because they see

nothing spiritually happening. Young people are hungry to see the fire of the supernatural power of God at work. God is raising up a group of young people who are willing to take the Bible at face value. Their attitude is if Jesus did it, then we can do the same.

2) We need the supernatural power of God in our lives to fight the devil. We cannot fight the devil with our natural abilities or intellect. The devil will eat you alive, chew you up and spit you out, if you are trying to fight in the natural. You can only come against evil forces in the supernatural. *The Apostle Paul said, "My speech and my preaching was not with enticing words of man's wisdom, but in demonstration of the Spirit and of the power of God, so that your faith will be in the words of men and not in the power of God,"* (1 Corinthians 2:4). If we're not operating in the demonstration of the Spirit's power, our faith will rest on human wisdom which is intellectual faith.

3) We need the supernatural to have a personal encounter or experience with the power of God. Theology (theory) or head knowledge is not enough, a lot of people have the knowledge, but they have not had an encounter or personal experience with the Holy Spirit, therefore, they are powerless.

4) We need the supernatural to become a carrier of the power of God to do ministry, evangelize, and share the gospel. If the supernatural is not present in our lives, God can't be glorified. *"God is Spirit, and those who worship Him must worship in Spirit and truth."* **(John 4:24).**

Some of us are tired of church as usual, the church is the only place people come not expecting anything. When we go to work we expect to get paid. We go to the gas station and we expect to get gas. When we go to the grocery store we expect to get groceries, but when we come to church we have no expectations. The time has come for the supernatural power of the Holy Spirit to become active in our lives. We should expect it every time we walk into our place of worship. If not, we need to find a church where we are being taught to walk in faith in the supernatural. Miracles can't happen in the natural, only in the supernatural. You should attend a church that expects miracles, signs and wonders, people to be saved, delivered, healed and set free in the name of Jesus. We are destined to walk in the supernatural. If the same power that raised Jesus from the dead lives inside of us we should be able to speak to some dead situations and they come to life. Start speaking to the mountains in your life by faith, and expect it to be removed. **Mark 11:23** says, *"For verily I say unto you, That whosoever shall say unto this mountain, Be thou removed, and be thou cast into the sea; and shall not doubt in his heart, but shall believe that those things which he saith shall come to pass; he shall have whatsoever he saith."*

Someone once said that there are three types of people, those who watch what happens, those who ask what happened, and those who make things happen. I don't know about you, but I want to walk in the supernatural where the Holy Spirit makes things happen, and He uses us to become movers and shakers for the kingdom of God.

If we are going to walk in the Spirit, reach our spiritual purpose, and emulate the New Testament Church, we have to tear down some strongholds in our lives. **Ephesians 6:12** says, *"For we do not wrestle against flesh and blood, but against principalities, against powers, against the rulers of the darkness of this age, against spiritual hosts of wickedness in the Heavenly places."* This scripture tells us that we are not fighting natural enemies. The spiritual wickedness in high places is in opposition to the believer, confirming we need the supernatural.

Do not conform to the world's standards because we are destined to walk in the supernatural. The Bible tells us to be transformed by the renewing of our mind. According to **2 Corinthians, 5:17**, *"...If any man be in Christ, he is a new creature: old things are passed away; behold, all things are become new."* Don't conform to the world's standard and terms, because you cannot conquer what you don't confront.

- The world says bipolar, but Jesus calls it a spirit of depression
- The world says they have issues, Jesus calls it sin
- The world calls it rebellion, Jesus calls it a demon of rebellion
- The world says sexual orientation – Jesus calls it sexual immorality

"You unbelieving and perverse generation," Jesus replied, "how long shall I stay with you and put up with you? Bring your son here" (**Luke 9:41**). Jesus referred to the disciples as unbelieving and a perverse generation because they lacked faith to heal the child. The disciples were powerless.

Learn to speak the supernatural power of God for supernatural provision, divine health, and financial blessings over your own life and over the lives of your loved ones. Declare and decree it daily! Prepare to live in Heaven on earth, which is that abundant life. We do not have to wait to die because God's will can be done on earth as it is in Heaven. Walk in the anointing of the Holy Spirit (the power of God), to do His work on earth (ministry).

I've been mandated to tell you that you don't have to settle for the ordinary, but instead prepare to become a super-naturalist – someone who walks by faith in the power and anointing of God. Someone who has the ability to believe the impossible, unreasonable, and believe that faith is now! Go ANYWHERE expecting the supernatural to happen and walk everyday expecting the supernatural, naturally.

Now the Lord is the Spirit, and where the Spirit of the Lord is, there is freedom. As children of the highest God we do not have to let anyone manipulate or intimidate us. Disciples have to be vigilant in the Spirit, praying always, because prayer has the ability to destroy anything coming against us. The enemy is designed to control, dominate, and manipulate you and your family by any means necessary to stop God's Kingdom. Cover your family with the blood of the Lamb. If you are tired of living in the natural and want to ask God to empower you to live in the supernatural, seek God. You have to believe that you are destined to win and walk in victory in the supernatural power of the Holy Spirit!

Know who you are in Christ and walk in that authority.

I HAD TO EXERCISE THE FOLLOWING VIRTUES
Chapter 11

- Love – I had to first fall completely in love with God, loving Him for who He is, and not what He could give me. Then, and only then, was I able to love my neighbor and my enemies with the help of the Holy Spirit.
- Prayer, Fasting, and Sowing Financial Seeds – I exercised these three spiritual disciplines directed by the Holy Spirit. Sometimes I prayed and communed all night long with God. I fasted for God to renew a right spirit within me. I sowed financial seeds because I understood the principle of seed time and harvest.
- Forgiveness – I had to make sure I did not harbor any unforgiveness in my heart for anyone. I knew if I did not forgive others, God would not forgive my sins. *"For if you forgive men their trespasses, your Heavenly Father will also forgive you. But if you do not forgive men their trespasses, neither will your Father forgive your trespasses,"* (**Matthew 6:14-15**).
- Faith – God taught me His saving faith. I thought I had faith, but God showed me that my faith was not in Him, but rather in the things I prayed for. My focus was either on faith itself or the THING I was believing for. In other words, I learned to put my faith to action by having faith in GOD, not by putting my faith in faith.
- Joy – In the midst of the storm, the joy of the Lord supernaturally became my strength.
- Peace – I had my mind focused on Jesus, which kept me in a place of serenity. When I was tempted to focus on my circumstances, I had to refocus on God through His Word, praise, and worship.
- Patience – One of the hardest virtues is to remain patient. I had to learn patience and wait on God for my deliverance.

- Rest and be still – I had to learn how to rest in God. *"Oh, sword of the LORD! How long will you be restless? Go back to your scabbard; be still; be silent!"* **(Jeremiah 47:6)** I had to find rest in the Lord and wait patiently for him.

Isaiah 40:31

As I studied **Isaiah 40:31**, I researched the characteristics of an eagle. Eagles are known for their strength, size, and gracefulness, keenness of vision and powers of flight. They are fast and can fly very high. Eagles are selective. They don't mingle with a lot of birds because they enjoy flying higher than most birds will fly. After God renewed my strength spiritually, I could run and not be weary, and I could walk and not faint. Then and only then was I able to fully understand and experience in Isaiah 40:31. You can too!

I challenge each of you today, regardless of what you are waiting on God to do in your life, get on a spiritual diet, exercise the fruit of the Spirit, and find rest in God. It will not be easy until you rely on the Holy Spirit to do the work in you. Ask God to strengthen and keep you focused on Him and what He is doing in your life. I promise you that God will renew your strength. You will mount up on wings as eagles. You will be able to run and not be weary. You will walk and not faint. Wait on God to bring about mighty works in your life. With God you are already a winner!

ABOUT THE AUTHOR

Joann B. Farlow is a graduate of St. John High School in Cameron, SC. She received her B.S. Degree from Claflin University, Orangeburg, South Carolina. She received her Masters of Education Degree from Lesley University and an Educational Specialist Degree from Walden University. She is a Business Technology teacher in the Orangeburg County School District.

Rev. Farlow is a Licensed and Ordained Minister at Unity Fellowship Community Church, Orangeburg, SC where she serves as an Associate Minister, Discipleship Class Facilitator, and Spiritual Leader of the Women's Ministry.

Her goal is to help others find the same intimate relationship with God and the revelation knowledge she has found- *"Everything we are praying for, we already have."* She wants others to know that God has so much greater for us. As we allow God to transform us, we position ourselves for the greater works Jesus said we will do in the Supernatural.

Rev. Farlow loves God and is a woman of prayer and faith. One of her favorite scripture is *Matthew 10:1: "And when he had called unto him his twelve disciples, he gave them power against unclean spirits, to cast them out, and to heal all manner of sickness and all manner of disease."*